THE JEWISH DIETARY LAWS

THE
JEWISH
DIETARY
LAWS

THEIR MEANING FOR OUR TIME
by Samuel H. Dresner

A GUIDE TO OBSERVANCE
by Seymour Siegel

THE BURNING BUSH PRESS
NEW YORK, N. Y.

This volume has been prepared under the auspices of the National Academy for Adult Jewish Studies of the United Synagogue of America. Its publication has been made possible through the generous cooperation of the National Federation of Jewish Men's Clubs.

FOREWORD

The word "kosher" is perhaps one of the best-known words in Jewish life. It has made its way into the English dictionary and is frequently found in colloquial usage. And yet, like most words used with great currency, its precise meaning is often lost in a variety of connotations.

The broader and more important term, Kashrut, is less well-known, although it is a concept central to Judaism. It is to this concept of Kashrut, of which the work kosher is but a part, that this volume addresses itself.

A perceptive observation regarding the American Jewish scene speaks of the revealing questions posed in different generations. It is said that the key question regarding Judaism several decades ago was "why?" The question in our own day, we are told, is "how?" In this publication, the basic mitzvah of Kashrut is dealt with from both these points of view, the "why" and the "how."

The meaning of the Jewish Dietary Laws is treated in Rabbi Samuel H. Dresner's perceptive and stimulating paper. Rabbi Dresner, the spiritual leader of Temple Beth El of Springfield, Mass., has prepared his essay to introduce the reader to the world of thought underlying the centuries-old institution of Kashrut. In it he traces the Biblical and Rabbinic roots of this fundamental of Judaism.

Rabbi Seymour Siegel, of the faculty of the Jewish Theological Seminary of America, has drawn up a concise guide to the observance of Kashrut, which constitutes the second part of this publication. While not intended to be exhaustive, it is indeed a helpful outline of the specific practices of Kashrut.

The National Academy is pleased to present this volume as one in its publication series. These publications serve as cogent statements of views held within the Conservative Movement and are not in the nature of official pronouncements.

The following colleagues graciously read the manuscript in whole or in part and offered valuable comments: Rabbis Ben Zion Bokser, Salamon Faber, Myron Fenster, Isaac Klein, Benjamin Kreitman and David Weiss. In addition, Mr. Jacob Neusner made a number of helpful stylistic suggestions. Our thanks are also extended to Rabbi Bernard Segal for his warm interest and to Mr. Moshe Sheinbaum of the Burning Bush Press for his assistance in preparing the volume for publication. We are especially indebted to Rabbi Jacob Milgrom for graciously making available material from his essay on Kashrut.

It is gratifying to note that a special printing has been arranged for distribution by the National Federation of Jewish Men's Clubs. The Federation's enthusiastic participation in this project has been a source of great encouragement.

We pray that this work may serve not only to introduce its readers to an understanding and an appreciation of Kashrut but will assist as well in the observance and practice of this basic mitzvah.

MARVIN S. WIENER, DIRECTOR
National Academy for Adult Jewish Studies of the United Synagogue of America

Nisan, 5719
April, 1959

INTRODUCTION

The National Federation of Jewish Men's Clubs operates in many areas, prominent among which is that of publications. Adult Jewish education has always been of primary concern to us and to further this program we have published booklets from time to time on themes concerned with vital Jewish living. In recent years we have made available pamphlets dealing with the Prayer Book, Ethical Living, the Sabbath, and Religion and the Prophets.

Kashrut has almost become a moot question in the lives of our people. It has only too frequently been overlooked and many even question whether the concept is valid for our day. What is needed is a modern rationale of Kashrut which will give our people an understanding of it and result in making it a part of their daily living.

The National Federation now takes great pride in presenting this larger work dedicated to the place of Kashrut in Jewish life. It is the hope of our Committee that this volume will be read, utilized for adult study groups, and will assist our people to gain a true appreciation of the place of Kashrut in Jewish life.

The National Federation of Jewish Men's Clubs is pleased to cooperate with the National Academy for Adult Jewish Studies of the United Synagogue of America in making available this work which is being published by the Burning Bush Press.

ARTHUR S. BRUCKMAN, CHAIRMAN
Committee on Adult Education

CONTENTS

THE JEWISH DIETARY LAWS:

Their Meaning for Our Time

by SAMUEL H. DRESNER

Preface

There is a well-known story about a rabbi who, upon coming to a new congregation, was taken aside by the president and in a friendly manner advised not to talk about certain topics from the pulpit: Hebrew Schools —because the children had to take music and dancing lessons and needed the afternoons for play; the Sabbath—because in America one was compelled to work on the Sabbath to make a living, and making a living came first; the Dietary Laws, Kashrut—because it was only an ancient health measure, out of place in modern times and, furthermore, too much trouble for the women to bother with two sets of dishes. The rabbi, surprised at the counsel he was receiving, asked anxiously: "If I cannot talk about Hebrew Schools and I cannot talk about the Sabbath and I cannot talk about Kashrut, what can I talk about?" The president replied in mild astonishment: "Why, that is no problem at all, Rabbi; *just talk about Judaism!*"

This story, bitter though it may sound, reflects a good deal of what has passed for Jewish life in the past decades in America. I say in the past decades, because matters have been changing considerably of late. And to the better. The concrete nature of Judaism is being more and more realized. We are coming to understand in an ever deeper fashion that our faith cannot be reduced so easily to a list of abstractions, that Judaism means Hebrew Schools, Sabbath and Kashrut. Jewish education, for example, has in the last ten years become a major concern of the American Jewish community. Tremendous efforts and vast amounts of money are at present being expended to raise educational standards, to increase student enrollment, intensify curricula and provide for better qualified teachers. The Sabbath, too, has undergone a national "revitalization" campaign through the auspices of one of the major Jewish movements in America. Books and articles have been published, classes in the observance of the Sabbath have been arranged and thousands of sermons devoted solely to this subject. But, while Hebrew education and, to a lesser degree but still noticeably, Sabbath observance have been brought to the attention of the American Jewish community, as yet, Kashrut has been consistently overlooked. The voice of that Synagogue president still dins in the ears of most of our leaders, and where the matter of Kashrut is concerned, they are mute. Rarely is an article written on the subject, rarely a sermon preached on the topic. It is ignored, passed over in silence, as if it did not exist, as if there were no crisis in Kashrut.

Of course, good reasons may be presented for this neglect. The movement away from Kashrut has been tremendous. No one will question the fact that there are far fewer Kosher homes in today's generation than in the past generation. Jewish leaders have been so busy attempting to achieve the simple task of Synagogue affiliation and some regularity in Synagogue attendance that a subject such as Kashrut, with all the difficulties and hardships it presents—apart from the lack of a satisfying modern formulation of its meaning and relevance—was virtually anathema. From a purely pedagogic point of view, then, it seemed wiser to devote the limited energies at hand to those aspects of Jewish life which promised easier and better results. And there is much to be said for this argument. Yet, we might well ask ourselves—even from the point of view of pedagogy—whether the time is not ripe for a facing up to this problem. There has been a return to the Synagogue on the part of our people. There is a mild renaissance of interest in things Jewish, especially in the area of religious values.[1] The real problem today is no longer one of membership. That has, to some extent, been achieved. It is rather a matter of deepening the religious consciousness of that membership, making it aware of Jewish teaching, bringing it to Jewish commitment, leading it back to the path of Jewish observance. American Jews have been told that they must belong to a Synagogue, but they have not as yet been told *what belonging to a Synagogue means.* Furthermore, if we look at the subject somewhat more closely, we can find scattered here and there small but significant numbers—growing numbers—of younger men and women who, discovering Judaism for themselves as something new and vital, and free from the prejudices which hampered their parents, have eagerly accepted Kashrut into their personal life, primarily as a means of identifying themselves with their people. The response to an intelligently conducted campaign, a call to Kashrut, sounded in our communities and congregations, may be more positive than we think. There is a spark in every Jewish heart which needs only to be kindled with insight and meaning. It is the purpose of this essay to contribute toward a modern rationale for Kashrut which will contain both of these elements.

I believe that the reasons for the diminished observance of Kashrut in our time are twofold: First, the lack of *knowledge about it*, and, secondly, the lack of the *will to do it*. Let us analyze the problem in that order.

I

THE PROBLEM OF UNDERSTANDING

Not Health but Holiness

Knowledge about Kashrut is, at best, minimal. It is more misunderstood than understood. The most common misconception regarding Kashrut is that it is an ancient health measure which may have had its place in antiquity but, what with modern methods of slaughtering, regular government inspection and sanitary food preparation, is quite clearly an anachronism which should be discarded along with the horse and carriage and the high-button shoe. But is health really the purpose of Kashrut? Of course, one must not overlook the concern for disease and the attempt to achieve purity in the Kosher laws; still we must ask the question again: is health the *primary* concern of Kashrut? Let us turn to the Biblical text for an answer.

In Leviticus (11:44-45), after we are told which animals, fowl and fish are permitted and which forbidden, the reason for this long series of laws is at last given: "I am the Lord your God; sanctify yourselves therefore, and be *holy*; for I am holy. . . . For I am the Lord that brought you up out of the land of Egypt to be your God; ye shall therefore be *holy*." In Deuteronomy (14:21) we read: "Ye shall not eat anything that dieth of itself . . .; for thou art a *holy* people unto the Lord thy God. Thou shalt not seethe a kid in its mother's milk." In Exodus (22:30): "And ye shall be *holy* men unto Me; therefore ye shall not eat any flesh that is torn of the beasts of the field: ye shall cast it to the dogs." Each of these passages deals with a different aspect of Kashrut and yet in all of them the same word is repeated again and again: *Kadosh*, holy. This, then, is clearly the purpose and the goal of the Kosher laws: not *health* but *holiness*.

To Be Holy Means To Hallow

What does holiness mean in Judaism?

There are three great spiritual forces in the world which can be distinguished in terms of their attitude toward such basic drives of man as hunger, sex and the will to power: Paganism, Classical Christianity and Judaism. Let us compare them in their broadest outlines.

Paganism glorifies these elemental powers as such.

Christianity subjugates them.

Judaism hallows them.

Paganism worships the forces of nature.
Christianity denies them as sinful.
Judaism serves God by means of them.

Paganism says nature is holy and thereby unleashes
the beast within man.
Christianity says nature is unholy and thereby frus-
trates the natural desires of men.
Judaism says nature is neither holy nor unholy, but
is *waiting to be made holy* and thereby sublimates
the natural desires of man through a system of
mitzvot, to the service of God.

It is well to begin this discussion by contrasting
Judaism with these two other major spiritual forces,
because, though formulated somewhat differently and
called by a variety of names, the pagan and classical
Christian points of view have dominated the thinking
of mankind down through the centuries, including the
twentieth. Strangely enough, though opposites, the
Christian point of view, by virtue of its very misunder-
standing of human nature, has often led back to the
pagan view against which it first revolted. Thus the
shocking ancient pagan glorification of sex as holy and
the perversions which resulted from this view brought
about the later Christian degradation of sex as sinful,
which in turn produced and still produces a constant
renewal of the pagan view. Sigmund Freud has written
at length about this causal relationship.

"Power" may serve as another example. History
knows both the glorification of the will to power in the
cruel tyrant or the greedy unprincipled citizen as well

as the rejection of this world (and therefore any manner of "power") for the monastery and the world to come as typified by the Christian saint or the holy men of the Eastern religions who train themselves to no longer feel pleasure or pain or desire and reject the actual society of men for an entirely spiritual existence called Nirvana. In the first case power is used to an evil end. In the second case—often a reaction to the first—power is rejected as being evil in itself, and society remains as it was.

The teaching of Judaism is categorically different. It maintains that our world is neither to be deified nor vilified, glorified nor subjugated, worshiped nor despised. It is to be hallowed. And herein lies the hope of mankind.

Martin Buber has expressed this unique approach of Judaism in a succinct fashion:

"Judaism teaches us to overcome the fundamental separation between the holy and the profane. This separation has formed a part of the foundation of every religion. Everywhere the holy is removed and set apart from the fullness of things, properties and actions which belong to the universal, so that the holy becomes a self-contained holiness outside of which the profane must pitch its tent. The consequence of this separation in the history of man is a twofold one. Religion is thereby assured a firm province whose untouchableness is always guaranteed . . . but the holy is not given a corresponding power in the rest of life . . .

"In Judaism . . . one need only note how many everyday actions are introduced by a blessing to recognize how deep the hallowing reaches into what is in

itself unhallowed. One not only blesses God every
morning on awakening because he has allowed one to
awaken, but also when one begins to use a new house
or piece of clothing or tool because one has been preserved in life to this hour. Thus the simple fact of con-
tinued earthly existence is sanctified at each occasion
that offers itself and therefore this occasion itself also
... The separation between the realms is only a provi-
sional one . . . In the Messianic world all shall be
holy . . . The profane is now regarded as a preliminary
stage of the holy; it is the not-yet-hallowed. Human
life is destined to be hallowed in its natural form. 'God
dwells where man lets him in!' The hallowing of man
means this 'letting in.' Basically the holy in our world
is what is open to God, as the profane is what is closed
off from Him, and hallowing is the event of opening
out . . ."

To Hallow the Everyday

This is why, according to one of the Rabbis of the
Talmud, the most important verse in the Bible is the
one from the Book of Proverbs, "Know Him in all thy
ways." The word to emphasize in this verse is *all.*
"Know Him in *all* thy ways." This means that we can
"know" God—that is, find Him and serve Him—not
only in the Synagogue or on the Sabbath, but in every
act, in every word, and in every place. It all depends
how we act and how we speak. It all depends on
whether or not we hallow that part of our life. Thus,
we may serve God by the manner in which we speak to
our wife, cast our ballot, fill out our income tax return
or treat our employee. In each case we serve Him by

hallowing the deed we perform, by making it a holy deed. We hallow the everyday by performing each deed so that it becomes a means of serving God. When there is love and devotion between husband and wife, marriage is hallowed; when we vote for the ability and integrity of a man and not the favors he may grant us, we hallow our country; when we deal fairly with our employee, we hallow our business. The duty of the Jew is to lift up all of life to God, *to hallow the everyday*, so that all of life becomes holy.

Indeed, it must be with the everyday, Judaism teaches, that we begin our task of hallowing. If we were to ask Christianity the question: how does a human being become holy, what is the mysterious process through which he attains this exalted quality, we would probably be told: by having the right feeling or thought, by possessing the proper creed or belief. Judaism would agree that feelings and beliefs are essential to holiness, but it would assert that the struggle for holiness on the part of a human being does not *begin* there (nor should it end there for that matter). Judaism is not a one-day-a-week religion, nor does it concern itself only with prayer or Synagogue or ritual, nor does it limit itself to catechisms. On the contrary, its great claim, as expressed throughout the entire range of its literature from the Torah to the latest responsum, is that it must encompass the entirety of a man's being; that it is, in fact, a way of life, affecting all of one's days or none of them, relevant to one's total manner of living or to none of it, just as concerned with the seeming trivialities as with the exalted aspects of one's existence. Indeed, it would assert that it is precisely with these seeming trivialities, these common, everyday actions of ours which are matter-of-fact and habitual and apparently inconsequential that we must commence, in order to create the holy man. And what is more common, more ordinary, more seemingly trivial and inconsequential than the process of eating? It is precisely here that Judaism would have us begin— with the everyday—claiming that it is more significant to learn how to prepare and eat our food than to reflect on a dogma, more important to say *ha-motzi* over a piece of bread than to memorize a creed. Make something fine and decent out of the common practice of eating and you will have achieved more than reading a whole library of books on theology. Man, Judaism seems to teach, is not so much what he *thinks* as what he *does*. Indeed, it would claim, proper thinking may well follow proper doing. Attitudes often derive from activities.[2]

Now we can better understand what the mitzvah of Kashrut is attempting to achieve and can see it in its proper context. We are commanded to be a holy people. "Thou shalt be holy for I the Lord thy God am holy." "Thou shalt be a kingdom of priests and a holy nation." Israel is commanded to be holy; again and again commanded to be holy. But how do we become holy? We become holy by making holy, by hallowing. We become holy by hallowing that which is not yet holy, the profane, the everyday. And it is through observing the mitzvot that we are able to hallow and be hallowed. That is the purpose of the mitzvot. Thus before performing any mitzvah we are bidden to recite a blessing which begins: Blessed art Thou O Lord our

God, King of the world Who hast *hallowed us by Thy
mitzvot. . . . (Barukh Atah Adonai Elohenu Melekh
Ha-olam Asher Kid'shanu B'mitzvotav. . . .)* Thus
the mitzvah of Kashrut was given to Israel in order that
they become holy. Israel is commanded to hallow the
act of eating, and through this making holy, become
holy. Judaism teaches us to hallow every aspect of life
through fulfilling the mitzvot. The mitzvah of Kashrut
helps us hallow the act of eating.

It is no simple achievement, however, this ennobling
of our way of eating. It is a function we have in common with the animals. And there are many who are
not greatly different from animals in this respect; they
approach it with the same gluttony and coarseness and
the same constant concern. Their meals are often
vulgar and disgusting. To sit at their table is an ordeal.
To hear as the central topic of conversation their discussion of food as served at this or that club, this or
that restaurant, this or that party, of the need for diet-
ing and the helpless habit of overeating, is appalling.
The descriptions we possess of Roman banquets and
the revolting excesses indulged in there certainly remind one of animals. Our modern displays may be
somewhat more sophisticated but are not really different in essence. The pagan glorification of elemental
needs is still very much with us. Thus, since man is
an animal and eating is a bodily function which he has
in common with the animal, he may likewise approach
his food as an animal—the only thought in mind being
how best to satisfy his desires. That is one attitude, the
pagan attitude. Conversely, the classical Christian attitude to the problem of food would lie in the denial of

the body and all its desires as so many necessary evils which must be tolerated. For it is not the body but the soul which matters, not this world but the world to come. Man is a sinful creature and cannot curb his lust; he is an animal and cannot obey God's law. Therefore the enjoyment of food is often looked upon by Christianity as sinful. Therefore the rigid manner of fasts which the church prescribes and the asceticism which has characterized the main stream of Christianity down to this very day.

Judaism, too, has a place for fasting among its tenets. But it does not see this as a solution to the problem of satisfying the desire for food. Thus we are not only commanded *to fast* on Yom Kippur; we are likewise commanded *to eat* on the day before Yom Yippur. As if to emphasize this, the sages wrote, "If one eats and drinks on the ninth day of Tishri (the day before Yom Kippur), it is as if he would fast on both the ninth *and* tenth days of Tishri." To this a later rabbi wisely remarked: "Thus we are taught that while it is difficult *to fast* for the sake of heaven, it is even more difficult *to eat* for the sake of heaven." Neither the glorification of the elemental drive for food as characterized by Paganism nor the ascetic view of eating as a necessary evil as characterized by classical Christianity. (One extreme has regularly caused a move of the pendulum to the other extreme in history. The reader may judge for himself at which point in the pendulum's swing we find ourselves today.)

Judaism teaches a third way. It says that God created the world and made man in His own image, that He has given man the power to discover God's will and to obey it, and that man's task, therefore, is neither to escape from the world nor to worship it as it is, but with Torah and the mitzvot to fulfill God's dream for His creation. It says we have the power to hallow the act of eating, that we can find a way of ennobling and raising this prosaic act which will lend it meaning and significance, an aspect of holiness, that we may even succeed in transforming it into a means of serving God. For man is not merely an animal, even a *rational* animal, as Aristotle would have it, an animal with a mind; he is better defined as a *religious* animal—an animal, yes, with all the functions and frailties of animals, but a "religious" animal, one which has the wonderful power to take his animal functions and turn them into something holy. The glory of man is his power to hallow. We do not live to eat; we eat to live. Even the act of eating can be sanctified; even the act of eating can become a means for achieving holiness.

Kashrut, therefore, may be defined as a part of Judaism's attempt to hallow the act of eating by teaching us reverence for life.

Eating Meat a Divine Compromise

How does Kashrut hallow the act of eating?

Kashrut teaches, first of all, that the eating of meat is itself a sort of *compromise*. To many it will come as a surprise that Adam, the first man, was not permitted to eat meat. Yet we have only to look closely at the Biblical text to see that this was surely the case.

And God created man in his own image, in the image of God created He him; male and female created

He them. And God blessed them; and God said unto them: "Be fruitful and multiply, and replenish the earth and subdue it; and have dominion over the fish of the sea, and over the fowl of the air, and over every living thing that creepeth upon the earth." And God said: "Behold, I have given you every herb yielding seed, which is upon the face of all the earth, and every tree, in which is the fruit of a tree yielding seed—to you it shall be for food!" (Gen. 1:27-29)

Thus Adam, the perfect man, as an inhabitant of the Garden of Eden, which represents the divine order of creation, the perfect, ideal society, is limited to fruits and vegetables. He is clearly meant to be a vegetarian. No mention of animals is made here as his food, only "every herb yielding seed" and "every tree in which is the fruit of a tree yielding seed." Not until we come to the story of Noah is meat permitted to be eaten.

And God blessed Noah and his sons, and said unto them: "Be fruitful and multiply, and replenish the earth. And the fear of you and the dread of you shall be upon every beast of the earth, and upon every fowl of the air, and upon all wherewith the ground teemeth, and upon all the fishes of the sea: into your hand are they delivered. *Every moving thing that liveth shall be for you; as the green herb have I given you all. Only flesh with the life thereof, which is the blood thereof, shall ye not eat!*" (Gen. 9: 1-4)

Adam is forbidden meat; Noah is permitted it. Why? What took place between the time of Adam and Noah to bring about this change? The answer is simple: sin. The law for Adam and the law for Noah both represent man: Adam in the Garden of Eden in his ideal state, Noah outside the Garden of Eden in his real state. Adam was not satisfied to live in the paradisal society. He rebelled against God and turned away from him. He wanted the flesh of living creatures for his food and was prepared to kill to obtain it. And so it was with his descendants. Man ideally should not eat meat, for to eat meat a life must be taken, an animal must be put to death. But man will eat meat. It is his desire and, perhaps, too, his need.

Just as at the beginning of time, in the perfect society as symbolized by the Garden of Eden, there was no eating of meat, so at the end of time, in the perfect society as described by the prophet Isaiah, there will be a return to the original state.

> And the wolf shall dwell with the lamb
> And the leopard shall lie down with the kid;
> And the calf and the young lion and the fatling together;
> And a little child shall lead them
> And the cow and the bear shall feed;
> Their young ones shall lie down together;
> *And the lion shall eat straw like the ox . . .*
> They shall not hurt nor destroy
> In all My holy mountain;

For all the earth shall be full of the knowledge of
the Lord,
As the waters cover the sea. (Isaiah 11:6,7,9)

Included in the prophet's description of the future
perfect society where all conflict within nature will
give way to peace and harmony is the fact that the lion
shall no longer live on the flesh of other beasts but like
the ox eat the growth of the field. And can we, therefore, not draw the inference that if the carnivorous
animal will disappear at the end of time, how much
more so the carnivorous man? If blood-thirsty animals
will themselves no longer devour other animals but
live on fruits and vegetables and even straw, how much
more so man? Man too, then, in the future time will
no longer eat meat. "The biblical account of the
scheme of human destiny represents it as a temporal
process with creation and the paradisal state at the
beginning and redemption in the Kingdom of God at
the end. In between is history." (Herberg) At the
"beginning" and at the "end" man is, thus, in his ideal
state, herbivorous. His life is not maintained at the
expense of the life of the beast. In "history" which
takes place here and now, and in which man, with all
his frailties and relativities, lives and works out his
destiny, he may be carnivorous.

Human consumption of meat, which means the
taking of an animal life, has constantly posed a religious problem to Judaism, even when it has accepted
the necessity of it. The Rabbis of the Talmud were
aware of the distinction between man's ideal and his
real condition, regarding food. Referring to Deut.

12:20, they said: "The Torah teaches a lesson in moral conduct, that man shall not eat meat unless he has a special craving for it, and shall eat it only occasionally and sparingly."[3] "Only one who studies Torah may eat meat, but one who does not study Torah is forbidden to eat meat."[4] "Once Rabbi Judah the Prince sat and taught Torah before an assembly of Babylonian Jews at Sepphoris, and a calf being led to the slaughter passed before him. It sought to hide itself in his cloak and began to cry, as if to say: 'Save me!' 'What can I do,' said Rabbi Judah, 'since it is for this that you were created?' It was therefore decreed in heaven that because he had no compassion, sufferings should come upon him. One day a weasel ran past his daughter and she wanted to kill it. He said to her, 'Let it be, for it is written, "His mercies are over all His works." ' So it was decreed in heaven that because he had pity, pity shall be shown to him. And his sufferings ceased."[5]

The Rabbis' awareness of the problem is again implied—in their discussion of Biblical traditions—in the manner in which they distinguish between *b'sar kodshim*, "holy meat," that which was first offered in the Tabernacle by the Israelites and only then permitted to be eaten, and *b'sar chulin*, "profane meat," that which was eaten even though it had not first been brought to the Tabernacle. This latter meat—*b'sar chulin*, "profane meat"—was permitted to the people after they had left the wilderness and entered the Land of Israel. It is, however, the term they give to this profane meat which is striking. They call it *b'sar ta'avah*, "meat of lust" or "meat of luxury," after the passage in Deut. 12:20.[6]

When the Lord thy God shall enlarge thy border, as He hath promised thee, and thou shalt say: "I will eat flesh," because thy soul lusteth to eat flesh; thou mayest eat flesh, after the lusting of thy soul. If the place which the Lord thy God shall choose to put His name there shall be too far from thee, then thou shalt kill of thy herd and of thy flock, which the Lord hath given thee, as I have commanded thee, and thou shalt eat within thy gates, after all the lusting of thy soul . . . Only be steadfast in not eating the blood; for the blood is the life; and thou shalt not eat the life with the flesh. Thou shalt not eat it. Thou shalt pour it out upon the earth as water. Thou shalt not eat it; that it may go well with thee, and with thy children after thee, when thou shalt do that which is right in the eyes of the Lord." (Deut. 12:20-21, 23-24)

The permission to eat meat is thus seen to be a compromise, *a divine concession to human weakness and human need*. The Torah, as it were, says: "I would prefer that you abstain from eating meat altogether, that you subsist on that which springs forth from the earth, for to eat meat the life of an animal must be taken and that is a fearful act. But since you are not perfect men and your world is neither a Garden of Eden nor the Kingdom of God, since your desires cannot be stopped nor your nutritional requirements altered, they must at least be controlled; since you will eat meat and since, perhaps you need to eat meat, you may eat it, but with one restriction—that you have reverence for the life that you take." "The flesh with the soul thereof, which is the blood thereof, shall ye not eat." (Gen. 9:4)

Reverence for the Life We Take

We are permitted to eat meat, but we must learn to have reverence for the life we take. It is part of the process of hallowing which Kashrut proclaims. *Reverence for Life*, teaching an awareness of what we are about when we engage in the simple act of eating flesh, is the constant lesson of the laws of Kashrut. Let us see how this is so.

Sh'chitah, the manner of slaughter. "Thou shalt kill of thy herd and thy flock which the Lord hath given thee, as I have commanded thee." (Deut. 12:21) This is the Biblical source for laws of *Sh'chitah* which are found in the Talmud and probably go back to Biblical times. The laws of *Sh'chitah* provide the most humane method of slaughtering animals. Great care is exercised that the knife to be used must be regularly examined before and after it is used to determine that it is perfectly smooth, without a notch that might tear the flesh. The cut severs the arteries to the head of the animal, thereby stopping circulation to the head and rendering the animal unconscious of all pain. This is not true when the animal is only stunned by a blow. The one who slaughters the animal, the *Shochet*, must be carefully chosen. He not only must slaughter the animal according to Jewish law but is obliged to examine its internal organs to make certain the animal was not diseased. Among non-Jews such positions in slaughterhouses are held, for the most part, by the lowest elements of society—tough, crude men. With

Jews it is otherwise. The *Shochet* must be both a learned and pious person. He must pass an examination attesting to his thorough knowledge of the laws of *Sh'chitah*. He must be a man of piety and is obliged to recite a blessing before he executes his duties, ever reminding him of the nature of his labor, that this whole process is but a "divine concession." Thus he is prevented from becoming brutalized by the manner of his work. ". . . Thou shalt kill of thy herd and thy flock which the Lord hath given thee, as I have commanded thee . . ." (Deut. 12:21); that is, we may slaughter an animal for food, but only "as I have commanded thee." Thus *Sh'chitah* teaches reverence for life.

"The commandment concerning the killing of animals is necessary," writes Maimonides in a similar vein, "because the natural food of man consists of vegetables and of the flesh of animals; the best meat is that of animals permitted to be used as food. No doctor has any doubts about this. Since, therefore, the desire of procuring good food necessitates the slaying of animals, the Law enjoins that the death of the animal should be the easiest. It is not allowed to torment the animal by cutting the throat in a clumsy manner, by poleaxing, or by cutting off a limb whilst the animal is alive. It is also prohibited to kill an animal with its young on the same day (Lev. 22:28), in order that people should be restrained and prevented from killing the two together in such a manner that the young is slain in the sight of the mother; for the pain of the animals under such circumstances is very great. There is no difference in this case between the pain of man and the pain of other living beings, since the love and tenderness of the mother for her young ones . . . exists not only in man but in most living beings."[7]

Kashering, the removal of blood. Through the process of *Kashering* the blood is removed from the meat. It is not enough that the animal must be killed in the most humane way, that the life of the animal is taken with care and concern, but even the *symbol* of life, the blood, must be removed. "Only be steadfast in not eating the blood; for the blood is the life, and thou shalt not eat the blood with the flesh." (Deut. 12:23-25; also Lev. 17:11; cf. I Sam. 14:32-34) To remove the blood is the purpose of the laws of *Kashering*. There is no clearer visible symbol of life than blood. To spill blood is to bring death. To inject blood is often to save life. The removal of blood which Kashrut teaches is one of the most powerful means of making us constantly aware of the concession and compromise which the whole act of eating meat, in reality, is. Again it teaches us reverence for life.

Limitation of animals to be eaten. Because we are permitted to eat meat only as a compromise, a divine concession to human weakness and need, animals which are *n'velah* (that which dieth of itself) or *t'refah* (that which is killed by another animal) are forbidden. Such animals have not been killed according to the Law, which procedure alone renders them permissible for food, since it alone attempts to reverence the life it takes. And only animals so treated may be eaten. Animals found to be diseased upon examination by the *Shochet* are declared *t'refah*. Furthermore,

only tame, domestic animals which are herbivorous
can be eaten. The especially fierce species of carnivorous fowl, such as the hawk and eagle, are forbidden.

The Larger Meaning of Reverence for Life

The lesson of reverence for life which the laws of
Kashrut teach has by no means been accepted in our
world where life, animal and human, seems to be the
cheapest of all commodities.

Only recently a discussion of the morality of hunting appeared in a well known magazine. One writer,
the distinguished critic, Joseph Wood Krutch, com-
mented that ordinary killers "are selfish and unscru-
pulous, but their deeds are not gratuitously evil. The
killer for sport has no such comprehensible motive.
He prefers death to life, darkness to light. He gets
nothing except the satisfaction of saying, 'something
which wanted to live is dead. There is that much less
vitality, consciousness, and, perhaps, joy in the universe. I am the Spirit that Denies.' When a man
wantonly destroys one of the works of man we call
him Vandal. When he wantonly destroys one of the
works of God we call him Sportsman." The zoologist,
H. E. Anthony, who defends hunting in the same discussion, admits "that a basic inconsistency underlies
the shooting of game . . .: no one will deny that there
is an inconsistency in cherishing a beautiful dog for
many years and going out every fall to shoot an equally
beautiful deer. But, so far as we know, there is no
escape from the tension of inconsistencies of which
life consists."

The reason why the world has never adopted the

opinion of a Mr. Krutch is because there has always
been a Mr. Anthony to throw up his hands in despair
and say that there is nothing we can do about it, that
man may be considerate to animals one moment and
take joy in destroying them the next moment, that the
feeling of kindness is countered by the urge to destroy:
that there is a killer instinct in man which cannot be
controlled. He might point to the so-called national
pastimes of cockfighting and bullfighting which draw
hundreds and thousands of spectators eager to see a
bird torn to pieces or an animal pierced with a blade.
And what of boxing in our own country, he might add.
If you watch the average crowd at a prizefight carefully, you will observe that when the fighters dance
about, feint and block, be they ever so skilled in the
art of boxing, the crowd is bored and grows restless.
They want to see some action; they want to see a
"killing."

The Jew is unable to look upon the sport of hunting
simply as an opportunity to get out into the open air,
flex his muscles and "renew his contact with nature."
He views the deliberate shooting of an animal for no
reason other than "sport" with utter abhorrence and
sees in it the aggressive instinct in man coming to the
fore. He knows that in the repeated act of killing, man
himself may become a killer. Judaism recognizes this
as a very real danger which confronts man. But it
neither offers pious platitudes of condemnation nor
does it confess helplessness. It has devised the laws of
Kashrut as a habitual system of spiritual discipline
which trains the Jew each and every day to have reverence for life, even though life must be taken to provide

him with food. By restricting the kinds of animals
which may be eaten, and providing for a humane
manner of slaughter and a trained slaughterer, we are
prevented from becoming brutalized by the killing of
animals for our food.

Reverence for life which Kashrut stands for finds
rich expression in Judaism. Many laws in the Bible,
for example, teach kindness to animals. Animals are
allowed to rest on the Sabbath (Exodus 23:12).
Ploughing with a bull and a donkey harnessed together is forbidden because they were not equal in
strength and the weaker would suffer in trying to keep
up with the stronger (Deut. 22:10). If a man finds a
nest of birds, he cannot take the mother bird and the
young; he first has to send away the mother to spare
her feelings (Deut. 22:6). While treading out the corn,
the ox (or any other animal) cannot be muzzled
(Deut. 25:4). When an animal is born, it is not to be
taken away from its mother for at least seven days. An
animal and its young must not be killed on the same
day, lest through thoughtlessness the young is killed
before the eyes of the parent (Levit. 22:26-33). The
Talmudic phrase, *"tzaar baal chayim"* (cruelty to any
living creature), which is considered a crime, has become a virtual folk expression among the Jewish people. Before one is permitted to sit down at his table to
eat a meal, the Talmud says, his animals must first have
been fed. Although the prohibition of not eating the
limb of a living animal was one of the seven Noachidic
laws, laws which the Torah proclaimed for all mankind, "today," H. Lowe points out, "eels are still
skinned alive, cod is crimped and lobsters are boiled

unpithed. It is remarkable that Jews did not kill animals for sport. Fish had to be netted. Mr. William Radcliffe in his book, *Fishing From Earliest Times*, blames Jews for lacking the sporting spirit. They caught fish by net; they did not play them with the rod. This is perfectly true. The word 'hook' occurs in the Bible only as a metaphor of cruelty, or as an instrument used by foreigners."

It is of significance to note that while the law requires a special benediction—"Blessed art Thou, O Lord our God, King of the Universe, who hast kept us in life, and hast preserved us, and hast enabled us to reach this season"—to be recited by a Jew upon putting on a piece of clothing for the first time, it makes an exception in the case of shoes, because they are made of leather. The life of an animal had to be taken to fashion them.

This, in fact, is the reason given in the *Siddur, Haminhagim,* for the prohibition against wearing shoes on Yom Kippur. "Rabbi Moses Isserles wrote: 'It is the custom to say to a person putting on a new garment, "May you wear it out and get a new one." There are some who write that one ought not to say this about shoes or clothing which are made from the skin of animals (even if unclean), for if that were the case, it would seem as though the animal were being killed to make a garment, and it is written, 'His tender mercies are over all His works.' Rabbi Moses Isserles also wrote that he who is slaughtering an animal for the first time ought to recite the blessing *shehecheyanu* when he covers the blood of the animal, not when he slaughters it; for he is injuring a living thing. Therefore, how can a man put on shoes, a piece of clothing for which it is necessary to kill a living thing, on Yom Kippur, which is a day of grace and compassion, when it is written, 'His tender mercies are over all His works'?"

One more word needs to be said about the lesson of reverence for life which the laws of Kashrut teach, perhaps the most important word of all. We have remarked that man possesses an aggressive tendency which the laws of Kashrut attempt to tame and control. But the matter does not end there, for the urge to kill in man, once aroused, may not stop with animals. Where does one draw the line between killing an animal and killing a human? To stalk a deer and hunt him down or to stalk a human being and hunt him down is not greatly different.

"The sight of blood, the rattle of death and the glassy stare contrive to dampen the joy of the first kill, if not to leave the initiate sick to his stomach. To kill for the first time may be an ordeal. Thereafter, however, the protest of the conscience is stifled: after repeated performances, compassion takes flight, love goes into hiding and other emotions fill the vacuum. The prospect of the hunt produces an exultation which henceforth is extended to the prospect of the kill. In the history of man, hunting began as a necessity: in self-defense or for food and clothing. But the means became an end: hunting for sport, to kill for the sake of killing, for the sheer pleasure of killing.

"Here is where the teachers of Judaism detected a danger to human society, claiming that he who brings death to a living thing willfully and wantonly is liable, under certain conditions, to bring death to the highest living thing, man. They spoke from personal experience. For they and their fellow Jews lived for centuries as lieges of hunter-sportsmen, and were not infrequently tortured, maimed and murdered with the same skills perfected in the hunt. Furthermore, in the course of their historical experiences, they saw the identical hunting skills applied to the greatest hunt of all—human warfare. And because they saw that war also was governed by gentlemenly rules—whether the Treuga Dei of the middle ages or the rules of the Geneva Conference of the past century—they felt justified in identifying war with the hunt, except that now the entire earth became the hunter's domain and its human occupants his most prized game."† Once the sense of reverence for life has been dulled, the conscience is blunted and the divine image in man obscured. The beast within him that has been chained and hidden then emerges with all his fearful power.

Is this not precisely what we have witnessed in our own generation and is this not the very danger that threatens the world today—that those who have no reverence for life will destroy mankind? Furthermore, is not the destruction of human life perhaps the most popular theme of the daily "games" which our children indulge in, gun in their hand and murder in their eye? Is not the destruction of human life the stock in trade of almost every comic book, movie or television program? The results of a recent study showed that

†Jacob Milgrom, "Jews Are Not Hunters," unpublished manuscript. I have drawn upon this provocative article at length in this section ("Reverence for the Life We Take"). Much of the material in the next session ("Why Ritual?") was likewise taken from the Milgrom essay.

over six thousand murders occurred on the television screens throughout the nation on a single day! This is the education our children receive two or three or more hours each day of the week. The incidence of juvenile delinquency—among which is juvenile murder—can be traced, in part, to the education to destroy which the average child cannot help but soak up from his daily games, the mass entertainment media and, even, the daily newspapers. We are living in an age when six million Jews could perish without great concern on the part of the world, because man's sense of horror has been blunted; an age which has invented a means of burning millions—the crematorium; a means of blowing up millions—the atomic bomb; and a term for annihilating an entire people—genocide. Was there ever an age which needed more the lesson of reverence for life?

There is hardly a more powerful or more effective means of teaching this lesson than the proper observance of the mitzvah of Kashrut, which is a daily education throughout one's entire lifetime, observed in the privacy of each individual home. *Kashering* and *Sh'chitah*, not to eat blood and a humane manner of slaughter, far from being outmoded are among the most up-to-date and relevant laws of our tradition. Indeed, if a new religion were to be created today, such injunctions might well be among the first to be promulgated for the needs of Twentieth Century man.

Why Ritual?

But is a specific ritual necessary to teach this lesson? Let us consider the matter. Thinkers today are concerned about how best to teach reverence for life, not only as a noble quality engendering kindness to animals but as a means of preserving our very civilization. Albert Schweitzer, the famous musician-theologian-physician, wrote thousands of pages about the solemn necessity of feeling reverence for life, which to him is the fundamental concept of humanity. Few people, it must be confessed, paid attention to him. When he left fame and fortune in Europe at the height of his success and settled in darkest Africa to found and personally direct a hospital in order to put to practice his belief and thereby bring it more to the attention of the world through his bold example, the number of his followers grew, and at the age of eighty he even received the Nobel Prize. But Schweitzer knows that with all his effort, he has succeeded in changing the thinking of only a handful of people and the lives of even less, and that when he dies, sad to say, what he stood for will probably die with him. Such is the way of man. Judaism, however, has always taught that words and human examples are good but not good enough. It claims to possess a surer way of bringing its great teachings into the heart and mind of every Jew. It is the way of the mitzvah. Jewish law, which is composed of the mitzvot, takes the great teachings of the Bible and fixes them into a regular pattern of observance which fashions a meaningful way of life, and through habitual repetition of this pattern and walking upon this way a higher kind of human being is created. The mitzvah of Kashrut is an eloquent example of this. Thus the reverence for life which Judaism teaches is not dependent on any one man or his admonitions, be his life ever so noble or his writings ever so wise. Kashrut is a systematic means of educating and refining the conscience of those who observe it from early age to death which continues in every age and in every country wherever there is a Jewish family and a Jewish home.

The observance of Kashrut by the people of Israel has helped to do precisely this for them over the centuries, for to teach reverence for animal life is, all the more, to teach reverence for human life. The Jews are called *"rachmanim b'ne rachmanim,* merciful ones and the children of merciful ones." The Talmud teaches that "man should rather be among the persecuted than the persecutors," and the Biblical reference to support this which is referred to, is one of the laws of Kashrut: that only animals which do not prey on other animals, such as the lamb or the cow, could be brought as sacrifices to the Temple. Have the laws of Kashrut contributed to the merciful nature of the Jewish people? "Consider the one circumstance," wrote A. Leroy-Beaulieu, "that no Jewish mother ever killed a chicken with her own hand, and you will understand why homicide is so rare among the Jews."

The majority of mankind agrees with the oft-repeated verse from the New Testament—"Not that which goeth into the mouth defileth a man; but that which cometh out of the mouth." But Judaism knows that what goes into the mouth can also defile a man, and thus it has created the system of Kashrut which has worked an untold good for the people of Israel throughout the centuries. The laws of Kashrut—which forbid the eating of blood, limit the number of animals which may be eaten and provides for a humane method of slaughter and a specially trained slaughterer—have helped to attain Judaism's goal of hallowing the act of eating by reminding the Jew that the life of the animal is sacred and may be taken to provide him with food only under these fixed conditions. From this he learns reverence for life, both animal and human.

Other people engage in diets for their bodies. We have created a diet for the soul. If the first is understandable, why not the second?

How We Eat

I remarked above that Kashrut—which teaches us that *the eating of meat is a compromise to human weakness and need and that we must therefore have reverence for the life of the animal which we take*— is only a *part* of Judaism's way of sanctifying the act of eating. This must be emphasized. Kashrut cannot be understood by itself; it is a part of something larger. Kashrut alone, therefore, is not enough. It is not only *what* we eat but just as much *how* we eat. And one cannot deal with the one without dealing with the other.

The Talmud says that the table upon which we eat is like the altar of the Temple. The whole process of eating is thus changed into a richly beautiful ceremony. We are bidden to wash our hands before breaking bread not simply to cleanse them—indeed, even if they already are quite clean, water must be poured upon them in the prescribed manner—but because the priests washed their hands before they offered a sacrifice. Salt is sprinkled over the bread with which

we begin our meal, because salt was put upon the
ancient sacrifice. And between the blessing over the
washing of the hands and the blessing over the bread
no word is spoken. Then the prayer, "Blessed art
Thou, O Lord our God, King of the Universe, who
bringest forth bread from the earth," reminding us
from whose goodness and lovingkindness our food
comes is recited. After the meal, Grace is said, thank-
ing God for having given us our meal and blessing the
members of the household. While Grace is recited, the
knife is covered, because no knife was allowed to come
upon the ancient altar, for the knife was a sign of war
and the altar a sign of peace. During the meal we are
told to speak words of Torah so that the children and
ourselves should be nourished not only by God's food
but by His word as well. Someone has remarked, and
wisely too, that a child is as much educated by what
he hears at his table as what he hears in his school
room. "R. Simeon said: 'If three have eaten at a table
and have spoken there no word of Torah, it is as if
they had eaten of sacrifices to dead idols. . . . But if
three have eaten at a table and have spoken there
words of Torah, it is as if they had eaten at the table
of the Lord.' "

Today we have no Temple in Jerusalem, no altar
there, no sacrifices, no priests to minister. But in their
stead we have something even greater. For every home
can be a Temple, every table an altar, every meal a
sacrifice and every Jew a priest. And what was for-
merly an animal function, a meaningless, mechanical
behavior, is suddenly transformed into an elaborate
ritual full of mystery and meaning.

Thus Judaism takes something which is common and ordinary, which is everyday and prosaic and ennobles it, raising it to unexpected heights, informing it with profound significance by laws of *what* to eat and *how* to eat, by teaching us that every act of life can be hallowed, even the act of eating. Abraham Heschel gave classic expression to this thought when he wrote that "perhaps the essential message of Judaism is that in doing the finite, we can perceive the infinite." In eating a slice of bread, we can discover God; in drinking a cup of wine we can sanctify the Sabbath; in preparing a piece of meat we can learn something of the reverence of life.

And so it is that in hallowing our eating *we* become hallowed, in making our habits holy *we* become holy. A whole people becomes holy—"a kingdom of priests and a holy nation"; an entire nation set apart for His service. Judaism is a way of life, which encompasses the kitchen and the dining room as well as the Synagogue. Not the glorification of man's elemental drives as in Paganism nor the unnatural subjugation of them as in classical Christianity and the Eastern religions, but the hallowing of them, the raising of them up to God, is the view of Judaism. The glory of man, it teaches, is his power to hallow. By means of this hallowing, he not only overcomes the beast within him but even surpasses the angels.

Concerning Abraham's receiving the three angels and preparing a meal for them, it is written, "And he stood *above* them,[8] under the tree, and they did eat." (Gen. 18:8) Puzzled by this verse, a disciple of Rabbi Zusya of Hanipol asked him if it was not strange that

Scripture should say that the man stood *above* the angels.

No, Rabbi Zusya explained. It was not strange at all. The angels are superior to man, but man is also superior to the angels. The angels are superior to man because they are pure and not a part of the natural world. Man is superior to the angels because, though he is a part of nature, he possesses the power to hallow and raise up to God the common, natural acts of which the angels know nothing. This verse is an example of that. The angels have no need of food and thus, even though they are pure, they are ignorant of the manner in which to hallow the act of eating. But Abraham was a man who knew that even by the way in which we approach our food, we can serve the Almighty. Thus, in this case when he invited them to his table for a meal, Scripture speaks the truth: he stood *above* them.

The man who finds his way to God in the midst of the world is greater than the angels. The angels may be pure because they are apart from our world; they come from heaven and are innocent of the tasks, the problems and vexations that confront man. They are static; they neither rise nor fall in their everlasting splendour. But man comes from earth as well as heaven; he possesses a body as well as a soul; he has evil thoughts as well as good ones; he knows passion and greed as well as justice and mercy. He is never static but rises and falls, is capable of turning into a beast or the most glorious of creatures. Man can be purer than the angels because he—and only he—is called upon to raise earth to heaven. Man can rise higher than the angels because his task is greater than theirs—to hallow all of life: to conduct his business with honesty, to be gentle with his wife and children, to fight for good government, to treat his fellowman as he would be treated, to curb jealousy and desire, to act in such a way that all his deeds become holy deeds, all his actions holy actions, even the commonest of them. Abraham stood above the angels because he knew something utterly unknown to them, namely, that eating may be hallowed by the thoughts, the intentions, the manners, the blessings and the preparations of the eater.

II

THE PROBLEM OF DOING

At the beginning of this essay it was stated that the decline of Kashrut observance in our time stemmed from two causes: lack of proper knowledge about it and lack of the will to do it. The first subject has, albeit briefly and inadequately, been dealt with. I have tried to demonstrate how Kashrut is part of Judaism's attempt to hallow the common act of eating and, therefore, why buying from a Kosher butcher who sells meat slaughtered by a *Shochet*, removing blood from the meat in preparing it for the table, saying a blessing before and after meals—why all this has relevance and meaning, lending holiness to a mechanical function and helping to produce a holy people. It is a matter of correct knowledge, of replacing false understanding with proper understanding, a matter of mind.

But there is something else involved in the problem of Kashrut, and that is the matter of *will*. The practice of Kashrut has to do with our will to live as Jews, with a decision that requires sacrifice and commitment, with a state of mind that is clear and decided. That is why the decline in Kashrut observance is so disturbing. It is not only a question of understanding—though this is central to the whole issue—but also one of determination, of the will to be a Jew.

To Be Holy Means To Be Set Apart

This second consideration, it should be noted, is likewise implied in the meaning of the Hebrew word for holiness, *K'dushah*, which the Bible constantly associates with the Dietary Laws. We have already said that the purpose of Kashrut was holiness and that holiness meant *hallowing*, in this case the hallowing of the act of eating. But the Hebrew word for holiness, *K'dushah*, has another meaning as well. It also means *to be set apart*. To be holy also means to be set apart. "I am the Lord your God, who have *set you apart* from the nations. Ye shall therefore separate between the clean beast and the unclean." (Lev. 20:24-25) The prohibition of certain kinds of fish or the separation of milk and meat, which is the outstanding characteristic of the Jewish kitchen and involves a goodly percentage of the laws of Kashrut, functions mainly to set us apart from non-Jews by providing us with a Jewish cuisine, Jewish kitchen and a Jewish table.[9]

Hallowing the act of eating is an acceptable concept to most people, but being set apart from others by virtue of this hallowing is not so acceptable. To many the whole idea of a democratic society in which ghetto walls are broken down and all peoples and faiths mingle freely and easily militates against such an impregnable food barrier as Kashrut. It is looked upon as a deterrent to good interfaith relations and was, therefore, one of the first parts of the Law which the early German Reformers dropped in their attempt to eliminate the non-universalistic aspects of Judaism. Indeed, even those who do keep Kosher homes do not hesitate to part company with these observances once they leave the privacy of their homes. "At home a Jew, in society a man," as the old Haskalah adage had it. Edmond Fleg, the distinguished French author, tells us in his moving autobiography, *Why I Am a Jew,* how, as a young boy, this double standard Kashrut of convenience drove him from his religion. "Once I was taken on a journey by my parents and at the hotel where we dined the fat and the lean were mixed, and cheese was served after meat. Even ham appeared on the table. My parents ate and permitted me to eat of this forbidden dish. Then the food forbidden at home was no longer forbidden when one was away from home? The law was law no longer?" Such inconsistency on the part of the parent is the surest way to guarantee that the next generation will abandon the Dietary Laws altogether. Such double standards can only be retained by virtue of an emotional nostalgia which is rarely, if ever, inherited. Either Kashrut is taken seriously as a means of singling Israel out as a people set apart for the Lord's service, every meal, therefore, being an opportunity to give witness to this fact, a regimen having significance not only in the confines of the home but outside the confines of the home as well, or it is doomed to extinction.

The tremendously alluring power of conformity as described by Riesman and others which sweeps together into the "accepted" pattern all dissident elements, all heterogeneous members, is nothing new to the Jewish people. It is an old ailment, whose bitter pain we have often felt. We call it, however, by a different name: assimilation, the desire to abandon one's distinctiveness and become like those around us. It is a constant temptation to the Jew: to give up the interminable struggle and go along submissively, indistinguishably, passively with the rest of the crowd. Furthermore, the distinction between inner-directed and other-directed persons, which the sociologists now use to describe those who act out of their own resources ("inner"-directed) in contrast to those who suppress their own feelings and conform to the crowd ("other"-directed), is exactly what we mean and have meant for centuries, when, discussing the Jews of Alexandria and Spain and Germany, we spoke of the assimilationists and the non-assimilationists. The only difference today is that the trend toward assimilation, that is, ridding ourselves of distinctive practices, is so much the greater in America because of the paucity of anti-Semitism and the overwhelmingly integrating factors of democracy. All this stands as a wall of protest against the practice of Kashrut, urging conformity, like-acting, like-speaking, like-eating, frowning upon anything in the way of thought or manner which might cause one to stand out from the crowd. Thus, it is not only a matter of understanding the meaning of Kashrut but also the will to do it that must be considered.

Kashrut in Jewish History

The people of Israel have possessed the will to observe the laws of Kashrut in the past. So strong has their will been to observe Kashrut that they considered it worthy of great sacrifice, even, at times, the greatest sacrifice. Consider for a moment the role which Kashrut has played in our history. At the time of the Maccabees part of the Greek persecution consisted in attempting to force the desecration of the Dietary Laws upon the Jews. The aged scribe Eleazar submitted to death rather than permit pig's flesh to pass his lips and is one of the first recorded martyrs of Israel. The record of the observance of these ritual prescriptions and of the self-sacrifice that was willingly undertaken for their sake is closely bound up with the whole subsequent course of Jewish history. Josephus tells us of the Essenes who, at the time of the great war against the Romans, "racked and twisted, burnt and broken, and made to pass through every instrument of torture, in order to induce them to blaspheme their lawgiver or to eat some forbidden thing, they refused to yield to either demand, nor even once did they cringe to their persecutors or shed a tear." Philo speaks of similar episodes in Alexandria. And so, too, in later generations, under different skies and in different circumstances. It is recounted how the Marranos of Spain risked their lives to procure meat that was Kosher and how this detail was considered one of the signs of heresy by the Inquisition, which sometimes brought them to their death. There is a record even of how certain of them, arrested by the Holy Office, managed to observe the Dietary Laws in the very dungeons in which they were immured. Thus a certain Francisco Maldanado da Silva, who was burned alive in Lima in 1639, refused to touch meat all the long years during which he lay in the condemned cell awaiting his fate; and this is not the only case. The same took place at the time of the Crusades when many Jews were dragged to the baptismal font but nevertheless clung to their ancestral practice. "It is fitting that I should recount their praise," writes a contemporary chronicler, "for whatever they ate. . . . they did at the peril of their lives. They would ritually slaughter animals for food according to the Jewish tradition." (Roth) Miraculous are the tales of Jewish boys who were forcibly taken into the Russian army at a tender age by Czar Nicholas, separated from their families, raised in distant lands as soldiers, beaten and starved to make them abandon their Jewish ways, and who nevertheless refused to eat forbidden food. To this could be added endless tales of spiritual heroism during the period of Nazi persecution of our own time. Apart from all these examples of endangering one's very life, is the day to day sacrifice which our people have made without question, complaint or any claims to heroics, in the ordinary course of their affairs: when they happened to be away from home on a trip or if they lived in a small village and had to travel many miles to purchase Kosher meat or the countless other cases in the ordinary life of the people of Israel when they

overcame difficulties in order to fulfill the mitzvah of
Kashrut. The weight of Jewish history regarding the
Dietary Laws weighs heavy upon us. The Talmud says
that those mitzvot for which Israel have had to suffer
have thereby become especially dear to them. The
mitzvah of Kashrut is undoubtedly included in that
group.

Particularism and Universalism

Perhaps we have been selling our Judaism too
cheaply of late, pruning it of all seeming unpleasant-
ries, hiding from the American Jew what the real
demands of our faith are, candy-coating it, making it
sweet to the taste, pleasant to the eyes, something that
gives a little brightness and color to whatever kind of
man you may happen to be. In a word: peace of mind.
The real challenge of tradition is glossed over; the
rigorous demands of the Law are rarely mentioned.
Instead, those aspects of the tradition are dealt with
which will arouse the least objection and the rest
studiously ignored. Kashrut is among that portion
which is ignored.

The truth is, however, that Judaism does make demands, stern, difficult—almost impossible—demands.
Judaism is a strict discipline which has produced—by
virtue of intensive and meaningful education and observance over a long period of years a special kind of
man and peculiar kind of people. Such results do not
come about automatically, from pious platitudes. Our
claim is not peace of mind; our claim is that the God
of Israel spoke to all mankind through Israel, that we
are His messengers to all the world, that the world

depends upon the truth enunciated in our tradition and that we are the keepers of that heritage for all mankind. Destroy the people and you destroy that heritage. For that heritage is not embodied in any book or idea (as with the Greeks) but in the people's living reality, the way of life which is tradition. We Jews are a narrow, nationalistic, self-centered people. There is no point in denying it. Only read the first part of the *Alenu* prayer which is recited at every Jewish service (except the Reform, which found its particularism too offensive):

> It is our duty to praise the Lord of all things, to ascribe greatness to Him who formed the world in the beginning, since He hath not made us like the nations of other lands, and hath not placed us like other families of the earth, since He hath not assigned unto us a portion as unto them, nor a lot as unto all multitude. We bend the knee and offer worship and thanks before the supreme King of Kings, the Holy One, blessed be He. . . .

The severe particularism of Israel is nowhere better expressed than in these words. They contain part of good Jewish doctrine. They declare our separateness, and our thankfulness for our separateness. But is this particularism an end in itself? Are we *only* particularistic? The answer to that question is found in the second paragraph of the very same prayer:

> We therefore hope in Thee, O Lord our God, that we may soon behold the glory of Thy might, when Thou wilt remove the abominations from the earth

and cause all idolatry to cease. We hope for the day
when the world will be perfected under the kingdom
of the Almighty, and all mankind will call upon Thy
name; when Thou wilt turn unto Thyself all the
wicked of the earth. May all the inhabitants of the
world perceive and know that unto Thee every knee
must bend, every tongue vow loyalty. Before Thee,
O Lord our God, may they bow in worship, giving
honor unto Thy glorious name. May they all accept
the yoke of Thy kingdom and do Thou rule over
them speedily and forevermore. For the kingdom is
Thine and to all eternity Thou wilt reign in glory;
as it is written in Thy Torah; The Lord shall be
King over all the earth; on that day the Lord shall
be one and His name one.

The loftiest, most universal utterance in our entire
liturgy is thus joined to the most particularistic. And
what is true of this prayer is true of all of Judaism.
Particularism and universalism go hand in hand. This
is the message of the Bible and the Talmud, the
prophets and the rabbis. We are a small, intensive
people which strives through much of its ritual to preserve itself; yet the end of this struggle is not simple
self-preservation—why be a Jew and suffer on that
account?—but to be a witness to God amidst the follies
and miseries of mankind, that the day might come
when the world would be perfected under the kingdom
of the Almighty, when every knee would bend and
every tongue pledge loyalty, when God alone would
rule, when He and His name would be one. Particularism and universalism, both are essentials of Judaism.

Destroy one and you destroy both. There have been times in Jewish history when the universal aspect of Judaism was almost forgotten, as is the danger in the land of Israel today. There have been times when the particularistic aspect of Judaism was almost forgotten, as is the danger in America today. In either case a fatal blow will have been leveled at the total Gestalt of the Jewish faith.

> Ye are My witnesses, saith the Lord;
> And My servant whom I have chosen.
> I the Lord have called thee in righteousness,
> And have taken hold of thy hand,
> And kept thee and set thee for a covenant of the people,
> For a light to the nations;
> To open the blind eyes,
> To bring out the prisoners from the dungeon,
> And them that sit in darkness out of the prison-house.
>
> (Isa.43:10; 42:6-7)

Holiness means *to hallow our lives*, but it also means *to be set apart for the Lord*. Thus one of the primary functions of Kashrut is to distinguish us from others, to separate us from the nations, to preserve us amidst the maelstroms of history. This must be said clearly and unashamedly. And such separation is just as necessary today in America as ever before. The logic involved is clear: if Judaism has a task in the world, then there must be Jews in the world. Otherwise there will be no Judaism. But the Jews are a small nation scattered amongst the peoples. How can they be pre-

vented from being swallowed up and assimilated in the
course of the years? Kashrut helps to separate them,
to distinguish them and preserve them, to remind them
three times a day who they are and what God chose
them to stand for, that all their days and hours—not
only certain days and certain hours—should be for His
sake. A gentile prophet spoke better than he knew
when he said of Israel: "Lo, it is a people that shall
dwell alone, and shall not be reckoned among the
nations." (Num. 23:9)

Kashrut is one of the firmest ramparts of the particularistic aspect of Judaism. It demands sacrifice,
self-discipline and determination—but what that is
really worthwhile in life does not? It demands the
courage to turn our face against the powerful current
of conformity that almost overcomes us daily, not only
against the gentile world as in the past (that was difficult enough, yet in doing so, one could always feel part
of an united people), but against the majority of the
Jewish world, thus standing witness to God amongst
our own nation as well as the "nations." Is this not,
however, what the prophet Isaiah—he who spoke of
his people as God's "witness" and "servant"—meant
when he sang of a "saving remnant" of Israel?
Throughout our long history—from Egypt to Palestine
to Babylonia to Spain to Germany to America—it has
always been that loyal "remnant," not the entire people, which has been faithful to our task and preserved
our heritage from generation to generation. Perhaps
we should thus describe the Jew who observes Kashrut
today as something different from the Riesman categories of "inner-" and "other"-directed. Perhaps we

should rather call him "tradition"-directed. It is the weight of the centuries which he carries in his soul that gives him strength, the yoke of the *halakhah*, the "way," which determines his course, the long chain of tradition to which he is bound and to which he yearns to add one more link, that guides his path—while before his eyes remains the glorious vision of the end of time when all nations will be one. Because he says "yes" to the glory and the grandeur of Jewish tradition, he has the courage to say "no" to the world with all its allurements and blandishments, with all its captivating call to conformity. The problem of Kashrut is very much involved with the will to live as a Jew.

To summarize, then, we may say that the goal of Kashrut is holiness, a holy man and a holy nation. It is a part of Judaism's attempt to hallow the common act of eating which is an aspect of our animal nature. It likewise sets us apart from the nations. Thus it achieves its objective, holiness, in these two ways, both of which are implied in the Hebrew word, *Kadosh*: inner hallowing and outer separateness. Finally, Kashrut makes two demands upon the modern Jew: understanding of the mind and commitment of the will. Both are indispensable.

According to Aristotle's pupil Clearchus, his master once had a discourse with a Jew and came away deeply impressed with two things about this people: their admirable philosophy and their strict diet.

Philosophy and diet, thought and practice, inner attitude and outward observance, *agadah* and *halakhah*—this combination has characterized Judaism since earliest times. It is the very essence of the Jewish religion.

A GUIDE TO OBSERVANCE

by SEYMOUR SIEGEL

After the discussion of the reasons for observing Kashrut we turn to the Dietary Laws themselves. No brief outline of these laws can be all-inclusive. A concise delineation of the main laws follows. If any unusual problem arises, a rabbi should be consulted.

DEFINITIONS:

Kosher or *kasher* means fit or proper to be used. *T'refah* is the opposite of kasher, as it is applied to food. Literally it means "torn by a wild beast" (see, for example, Exodus 22:30). The term *t'refah* has been extended to include other foods deemed objectionable by Jewish tradition.

KEEPING A KOSHER HOME

I. PERMITTED FOODS: The classes of permitted foods are:

1. All fruits and vegetables.

2. All animals which part the hoof and are cloven-footed and chew the cud; such as cattle, sheep, goats.

3. All sea food that has fins and scales. This means that eel, shark, shellfish such as oysters, crab, and lobsters cannot be eaten. In addition, the roe of non-Kosher fish are not permitted. According to a ruling of the Rabbinical As-

sembly of America's Committee on Law and Standards, sturgeon and swordfish are Kosher.

4. Most domesticated fowl such as chickens, most species of duck and geese, turkey, pigeon and squab. Only eggs from Kosher fowl may be eaten.[1]

II. PURCHASE OF RITUALLY-SLAUGHTERED MEAT: In addition to choosing foods from the categories of I above, the Dietary Laws require the following: If the food is meat or fowl, it must be slaughtered properly. (This does not apply to fish.) It should be bought from a butcher who sells meat which has been slaughtered according to Jewish law.[2]

III. KASHERING MEAT: If the food is either animal or fowl it must be kashered. That is to say, the blood is to be removed from the meat. In many communities, the butcher will do this for you. However, if you *kasher* the meat yourself the following rules should be observed:

1. The meat (this includes bones) should be rinsed thoroughly with water.

2. The meat is then soaked for a half hour; the water should cover all the meat. (In an emergency, a shorter period of time is permissible.)[3]

3. The vessel which is used to soak the meat should not be used for any other purpose.

4. After the meat has soaked for a half hour, it is to be removed from the water and placed

on a smooth, grooved, incline or else on a perforated surface. This is done so that the blood may drain off.

5. Salt is spread on the meat, covering all sides so that no spot remains without salt. Therefore, poultry must be opened before salting so that it can be sprinkled on the inside.

6. The salt used should not be fine, for in that case it would melt immediately and would not purge the blood from the meat. On the other hand it should not be too coarse, lest it fall off the meat. It should be medium-coarse. Most markets carry salt which is certified "proper to be used for kashering."

7. Poultry should be placed on the salting board with the inside part downwards so that the blood will not accumulate on the inside.

8. All inside parts of the fowl should be removed before salting. They should be salted separately.

9. The gizzard should be cut open and cleaned before kashering.

10. The meat should remain in salt for about an hour. (In an emergency, a shorter period of time is permissible.)[4]

11. After the meat has lain in its salt, it is customary to rinse it three times in clear, cold water.

12. The heart and the liver require the following procedure:

a. Before salting the *heart*, it is customary to cut off the tips, slice open the remaining part and remove the accumulated blood.

b. The *liver* has much blood. Therefore, the blood cannot be removed from it through salting. It is necessary to broil it in fire. This procedure is described in detail in the section on broiling.

Some General Rules to Remember:

1. Fowl may not be placed in boiling or hot water for cleaning purposes before it is kashered. This would tend to coagulate the blood so that it would be impossible to purge it by soaking and salting.

2. Meat should not be ground before it has been kashered. A grinder used for un-kashered meat may not be used for kashered meat.

3. Meat should not be frozen for subsequent use unless it has been kashered. There are certain emergency situations when this rule can be relaxed. (This rule, however, does not apply when the meat is to be broiled.) If there is any question, a rabbi should be consulted.

IV. BROILING: Broiling is considered to be the most powerful agent for the removal of blood from meat. Therefore, when the meat is broiled it is not necessary to *kasher* the meat as described above. The following rules should be observed:

1. Before broiling, the meat should be rinsed and all surface blood removed.

2. A small amount of koshering salt should be sprinkled on the meat immediately before broiling.

3. As mentioned above, liver cannot be kashered in the ordinary way because it contains a great amount of blood. It can be prepared for eating only through broiling. If it is desired to fry the liver or prepare it in some other way the liver should first be broiled over the flame long enough so that there is a change of color and a crust has been formed. The accumulated blood should be rinsed off. After this, the liver may be cooked or fried.

4. Unkashered (that is, not kashered through salting and soaking) chopped meat should not be broiled if other ingredients such as eggs or flour are present in the meat.

5. Broiling should be done only on a grid which allows the blood to drip freely from the meat as it is cooking. The pan into which the blood drips should not be used for any other purpose.

6. An electric broiler has the same status as any other broiler.[5]

V. THE LAWS OF "MEAT AND MILK": In addition to the laws of kashering or broiling, care must be taken in regard to cooking and serving, as well.

This involves mainly the laws of "Meat and Milk."[6]

The following are the rules to keep in mind:

A. Eating "Meat and Milk"

1. No meat and milk products may be eaten together in the same meal. Special care should be taken in regard to bread and cake. The ingredients should be carefully noted so that a product containing milk or butter *(milchig)* will not be served with meat or meat products *(fleishig)*.

2. After eating meat it is customary to wait until the next meal before eating dairy products. Customs differ as to how long this requires. Three hours has been the custom of the German and most West European Jews; six hours for East European Jews; 72 minutes is the prevailing custom among Dutch Jews.[7]

3. After dairy foods, meat foods may be eaten without waiting. However, Grace After Meals should be recited, the mouth rinsed and the tablecloth changed.

4. Because hard cheeses adhere to the teeth, it is the opinion of many authorities that after eating them, the "between meals" interval should be observed before eating meat products.

5. Fruits, vegetables, fish, and eggs are *pareve*, that is "neutral." They are considered to be neither milk nor meat.

B. Cooking "Meat and Milk"

Dishes and pots, even when they are glazed, absorb the taste of the foods cooked and eaten in them. Therefore, it is not only prohibited to cook meat and milk products together in the same pot, but if a pot or dish has once been used for meat it may not be used for milk and vice versa. That is why at least two sets of pots and pans, silverware, and dishes are required in a Jewish home. Here are some important rules to remember:

1. Meat and dairy utensils should not be washed together.

2. It is advisable to have clearly-marked dishtowels and dishcloths (usually by separate colors) for meat and dairy. It is best to store meat dishes and silverware separate from dairy dishes and silverware.

3. It is not proper to cook both dairy products and meat in a closed oven, on a range, or on an open gas stove without covering the pots in which they are cooked.

VI. OTHER RULES TO REMEMBER:

1. *Blood Spots in Eggs:* It is prohibited to eat any manner of blood. Therefore, if a speck of blood is found in an egg, the egg should not be used.

2. *Glass Dishes:* According to some authorities, glass dishes are not absorbent. Therefore, they could be used for both milk and meat. Other authorities hold them to be absorbent

and forbid such use. The Rabbinical Assembly's Committee on Law and Standards recommends that wherever possible, the same set of glass dishes *not* be used for both meat and dairy. The ruling is based on the fear that this practice might lead to carelessness in regard to other utensils.[8]

3. *Dishwashers:* An electric dishwasher may be used for both meat and dairy utensils. The following rules should be followed:

a. Meat and dairy dishes should not be washed at the same time.

b. Hot water should be allowed to run through the empty dishwasher after it has been cleaned and before washing another set of dishes.

c. Most authorities require separate trays. There are some who do not require separate trays if they are metal. However, all agree that if the trays are plastic, there should be one for meat and another for dairy.

4. *Washing Dishes:* Meat and dairy dishes should not be washed together in the same sink. It is well to have two separate sinks. If such facilities are not available, the dishes should be placed on separate meat or dairy trays made of wood, metal, or rubber. Only Kosher soaps or detergents should be used.

5. *Canned or Packaged Foods:* In shopping, care should be given to the ingredients in canned or prepared foods. Shopping is made easier by the practice of many food processors of preparing their products under rabbinic supervision, which is indicated on the label. Shortenings other than vegetable products should be avoided. (It may be assumed that if the word "shortening" without any qualification appears on a label, it is not a vegetable shortening and hence cannot be used.)

VII. PASSOVER AND ITS OBSERVANCE[9]

An important part of the Passover observance is the traditional practice of thoroughly cleansing the home and the removal of all *chametz* or leaven. Jewish law calls for the meticulous avoidance of *chametz*—even in minute quantity —throughout the Passover days, both at home and away.

The prohibition of *chametz* applies not only to certain foods, the use of which is to be avoided during *Pesach*, but also applies to the dishes and utensils in which foods are prepared or served during the year. These dishes or utensils may not be used during *Pesach* except as herein indicated.

A. Foods During Pesach

1. *Forbidden for use:* The following foods are forbidden for use during *Pesach:* Bread, leavened cakes, biscuits and crackers, cereals,

coffee substances derived from cereals, wheat, barley, oats, rice, dry peas and dry beans, and all liquids which contain ingredients or flavors made from grain alcohol.

2. *Permitted Foods:*

   a. *If Certified for Passover use by Rabbinical Authority:*

   Matzot, matzah flour, Passover noodles, candies, cakes, beverages, canned and processed foods, milk, butter, jams, cheese, jellies, relishes, dried fruits, salad oils, vegetable gelatin and shortenings, vinegar, wines and liquors.

   Labels and tags marked "Kosher L'Pesach" are of no value unless they bear rabbinical signature.

   b. *Requiring No "Kosher L'Pesach" Label:*

   Fresh fruits and vegetables (except peas and beans, but string beans are permitted). Fruits and those vegetables normally permitted for Passover use are permitted in their frozen state if they are not pre-cooked or processed. The following foods are permitted if they are in unopened packages or containers: natural coffee, sugar, tea, salt, pepper.

   B. Dishes and Utensils

1. Only dishes and utensils specially reserved for Passover should be used. The following are the exceptions to this general rule:

a. The silverware, knives, forks and spoons made wholly of metal used during the year may be used on Passover if thoroughly scoured and then immersed in boiling water. It is customary to follow this immersion with rinsing in cold water. All table glassware is permitted after soaking for 72 hours, changing the water each 24 hours. Fine translucent chinaware, if not used for a year, is permitted.

b. Metal pots and pans used for cooking purposes only (but not for baking), if made wholly of metal, though used during the year, may be used on Passover. They require thorough scouring to be followed by immersion in boiling water.

c. Utensils used for baking during the year cannot be used during Passover because of the great difficulty involved in kashering such utensils.

2. Earthenware, enamelware and porcelain utensils used during the year may not be used on *Pesach.*

3. The stove is prepared for *Pesach* by thoroughly scrubbing and cleansing all parts and turning on full flame in the bake oven and all the grates (until the grates are red-hot).

4. A dishwashing machine may be used for Passover after thorough scouring with boiling water. A new tray is required however.

Owing to the complexity of the Passover laws, it is advisable to consult a rabbi in case of doubt.

EATING OUTSIDE THE HOME

Owing to the small number of Kosher dining facilities available in the United States and Canada, situations frequently arise in which it may be necessary to relax the strict standards of Kashrut observed in the home.

When a person finds himself in such a predicament, the following principles should be used as a guide:

1. A thorough investigation should be made to ascertain that there are in fact *no* Kosher facilities available. These facilities might be found in vegetarian or dairy restaurants.

2. If it is necessary to dine in non-Kosher establishments, it is best to avoid all cooked foods. It is the view of some who observe Kashrut to sanction the eating of cooked foods if the food contains no forbidden ingredients.

3. A difficult situation, such as that of a member of the peacetime Armed Forces, may necessitate the eating of cooked foods generally. In such an instance, all dishes containing non-Kosher meat should be avoided.

OTHER TRADITIONS REGARDING EATING

The Jewish home is sanctified by the observance of Kashrut. In addition to the steps listed above, the table itself becomes an altar of holiness. In order to realize this goal Jewish tradition has prescribed the following:

1. *Ritual Washing of the Hands:* Washing the hands is not only an hygienic measure. It is also a religious ceremony. Therefore a special blessing has been ordained to be recited immediately before drying the hands. The water should be poured on the hands from a glass or some other vessel. The blessing is:

Barukh Atah Adonai, Elohenu Melekh ha-olam, asher kid'shanu b'mitzvotav, v'tzivanu al n'tilat yadayim.

Praised be Thou, O Lord our God, King of the universe, who has sanctified us through Thy commandments and commanded us concerning the washing of the hands.

2. *The Blessing over the Bread:* Immediately after washing the hands, (without any interruption, even of talking) a blessing should be pronounced over the bread:

Barukh Atah Adonai, Elohenu Melekh ha-olam, ha-motzi lechem min haaretz.

Praised be Thou, O Lord our God, King of the universe, who bringest forth bread from the earth.

If one pronounces this blessing it is not ordinarily necessary to pronounce any other blessing during the meal.

3. *Grace After Meals:*

   a. After the meal, Grace is recited.

   b. Prior to the recitation of the Grace, it is customary to remove any knives which happen to be on the table.

   c. It is also customary to leave some bread crumbs on the table during Grace.

   d. It is preferable to have at least three persons say Grace together.

NOTES TO
THE JEWISH DIETARY LAWS:
Their Meaning For Our Time

[1] See Nathan Glazer's *American Judaism* (University of Chicago Press, 1957) and Will Herberg's *Protestant, Catholic, and Jew* (Doubleday, 1955).

[2] This does not mean that Judaism is simply a religion of *halakhah*, advocating only the keeping of the law as a kind of "sacred physics" (Abraham J. Heschel), without concern for principles. Indeed, the mechanical observance of the laws of Kashrut without any proper understanding of what one is about, of the meaning of what one is doing —as, unfortunately, is all too often the case—is a denial of the very purpose of the Torah. One can obey the Law meticulously, wrote Nachmanides, and yet be a hateful person. Likewise, he might well have added, one can obey all the regulations of Kashrut and yet be a glutton. Doing must lead to thinking and activity to attitude. Concern for the spirit is equally a part of Judaism.

[3] Chulin 84a

[4] P'sachim 49b

[5] B'reshit Rabah 33:3
Bava M'tzia 85a

[6] Moses had difficulty restraining the craving of the Hebrews for the "flesh pots" of Egypt. Nor did the heavenly manna satisfy their appetites. Thus Moses was forced to arrange a flesh meal for the evening (Yoma 75b). Again, the rabble among them "fell a-lusting" and demanded more meat (Num. 11:4). They were then supplied in good measure with quails from the sea, which, however, caused an epidemic (Num. 11:31-34; comp. Ps. 128: 25-31).

[7] *Guide of the Perplexed*, Friedlander translation, Part III, Chapter 48, p. 253.

[8] The Hebrew word is *alehem.*

⁹ This does not mean that "reasons" have not been given for the separation of milk and meat. The Targum already understood the verse "Thou shalt not cook a kid in its mother's milk," in this larger sense. According to Maimonides the Biblical prohibition had its origin in the fact that the pagan cults of Canaan practiced a fertility rite which was particularly abominable and which revolted the Jews: the cooking of a kid in its mother's milk. Another "reason" advanced by Dr. Abraham J. Heschel for the prohibition may be that the goat—for us more commonly the cow—generously and steadfastly provides man with the single most perfect food he possesses: milk. It is the only food which, by reason of its proper composition of fat, carbohydrate and protein, can by itself sustain the human body. How ungrateful and callous we would be to take the child of an animal to whom we are so indebted and cook it in the very milk which nourishes us and is given us so freely by its mother.

NOTES TO
A GUIDE TO OBSERVANCE

¹ The Bible does not give us any general principles by which to distinguish the Kosher from the non-Kosher fowl. But the Bible does contain lists of specific fowl which can be eaten. From these lists the Talmud derives that permitted birds must possess the following characteristics:

   a. they cannot be birds of prey;

   b. they should not have a front toe;

   c. they must have a craw; their stomachs should have a double skin which can be easily separated;

   d. they must catch food thrown into the air, but lay it upon the ground and tear it with their bills before eating.

² The Jewish method of slaughtering *(sh'chitah)* is a method designed to cause the animal the least pain; to bring

about instant death; and to remove as much blood as possible. It consists of cutting the throat of the animal with a single swift and uninterrupted horizontal sweep of a knife (which must be sharper and smoother than a surgical knife) in such a manner that the knife cuts across the throat and severs the trachea, esophagus, carotid arteries and jugular vein. The knife-blade must be perfect, without the least perceptible nick.

[3] See *Ramo* on *Shulchan Arukh, Yoreh Deah* 69:1.

[4] See *Shulchan Arukh, Yoreh Deah* 69:6.

[5] Report of the Committee on Jewish Law and Standards of the Rabbinical Assembly of America, 1953 Proceedings, p. 40.

[6] The Bible notes in three places "Do not seethe a kid in its mother's milk." This has been interpreted by the rabbis in the Talmud as referring to the mixing of *any* meat product with *any* milk product.

[7] See *Chulin* 105a, and *Shulchan Arukh, Yoreh Deah* 89:1.

[8] *Avot d'Rabbi Nathan*, Version A, Chapter 41; Responsa of the *Rashba*, #233; *Shulchan Arukh, Orach Chayim* 451:26.

[9] The Committee on Jewish Law, Philadelphia Branch of the Rabbinical Assembly of America, prepared a statement on Passover observance which was subsequently revised and approved by the Committee on Jewish Law and Standards of the Rabbinical Assembly. This statement served as a basis for section VII of this guide.

INDEX

Abraham, and the three angels, 41–42

Adam, as a vegetarian, 21

Africa, Albert Schweitzer in, 37

Agadah, 54

Alcohol, grain, forbidden for Passover, 64

Alenu prayer, 50

Alexandria, Jews of, 46–47

American Jewish community, 10

American Judaism, 69

Animals, blood of, as sacred, 33, 39; bull, 32; cattle, permitted, 38, 55; clean vs. unclean, 44; with cloven hoof, 55; cud-chewing, 55; domestic and herbiverous, 30; donkey, 32; goat, permitted, 55; kindness to, in Jewish law, 32, 37; lamb, permitted, 38; limbs of living, 32; *n'veleh*, 29; organs of, 27, 57; permitted or forbidden for food in Jewish law, 13, 29, 32, 38–39; reverence for, in Jewish law, 26; slaughter of, in Jewish law, 27; Torah on, 26; *t'refah*, 29; *see also* Killing; *Sh'chitah*

Anthony, H. E., on hunting, 30–31

Anti-Semitism, in America, 46

Aristotle, 54; on man, 21

Asceticism, Christian, 20; *see also* Christianity

Assimilation, among Jews, 46; *see also* Conformity

Atomic bomb, 36

Avot d'Rabbi Nathan, 62, 71

Babylonia, Jews of, 53

Benediction, for clothing, 33; excepting shoes, 33

Bible, on animals, 32; on Kosher vs. non-Kosher fowl, 70; on separation of milk and meat, 13, 55, 71; teachings of, 37

Biblical references: *Deuteronomy 12: 20–21*, 24–25, 27–28; *12:23–25*, 29; *14:21*, 13; *22:6*, 32; *22:10*, 32; *25:4*, 32; *Exodus 22:30*, 13, 55; *23:12*, 32; *Genesis 1:27–29*, 22; *9:4*, 27; *18:8*, 41; *Isaiah 11:6–7*, 9, 23–24; *42:6–7*, 52; *43:10*, 52; *Leviticus 11:44–45*, 13; *17:11*, 29; *20:24–25*, 44; *22:26–33*, 32; *22:28*, 28; *Numbers 11:4*, 69; *11:31–34*, 69; *23:9*, 53; *Psalms 128:25–31*, 69; *I Samuel 14:32–34*, 29

Birds, with craw, 70; with front toe, 70; kindness to, 32; permitted for food, 70; of prey, 70; *see also* Fowl

Biscuits, forbidden for Passover, 63

Blessing, after meals, 43; over bread, 40, 67; of the household, 40, 43, 67; Kiddush, 18–19; *shehecheyanu*, 33; *see also* Grace; *Ha-motzi*

Blood, in eggs, 61; as life, 29; prohibition against eating in Jewish law, 29,

72